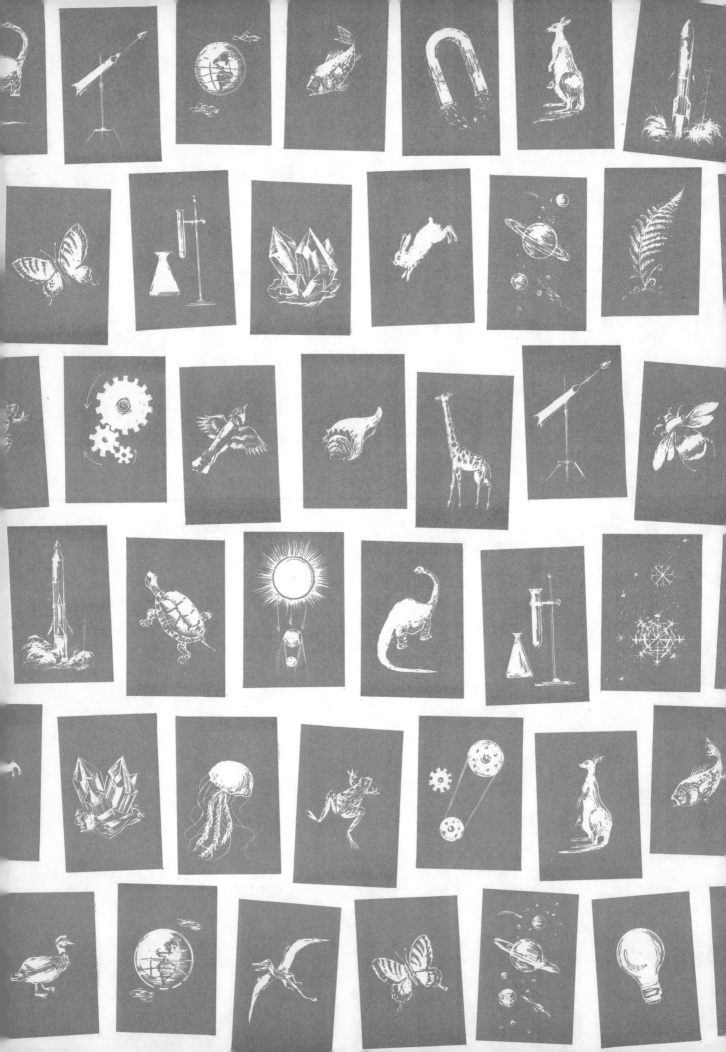

THE HOW AND WHY WONDER BOOK OF
EXPLORATIONS
AND DISCOVERIES

Written by
IRVING ROBBIN

Illustrated by
DARRELL SWEET

Editorial Production:
DONALD D. WOLF

Edited under the supervision of
  Dr. Paul E. Blackwood
  Specialist for Elementary Science
  U. S. Department of Health, Education and Welfare
  Washington, D. C.

Text and illustrations approved by
  Oakes A. White
  Brooklyn Children's Museum
  Brooklyn, New York

GROSSET & DUNLAP • Publishers • NEW YORK

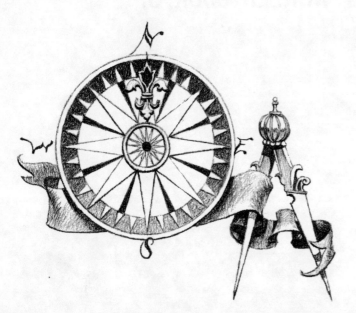

Introduction

There are several interesting ways to read *The How and Why Wonder Book of Explorations and Discoveries.* You can read it to find out why people have wanted to explore new and strange parts of the world. Was it for food, land, riches or sheer adventure? Or you can read it to find out who were the leading explorers of the past. Marching through the pages of this book are the great explorers of all time — Leif Ericsson, Marco Polo, Columbus, Balboa and many others. You may read to learn how ancient and modern explorations and discoveries have changed the course of history, or to see how man's knowledge of his world gradually expanded.

Perhaps you may wish to read to find out how new methods of travel and new inventions played a part in discovery. Why, for example, did we have to wait until 1958 to make a trip under the ice cap of the North Pole? How was the *Nautilus* different from Henry Hudson's *Half Moon?*

When you read *The How and Why Wonder Book of Explorations and Discoveries,* you will catch the spirit and the urgency that men have always felt to explore the unknown. And though everyone cannot be a Columbus or an Admiral Byrd, there are still frontiers in the ocean depths and in outer space yet to be explored and discoveries to be made in the universe by modern adventure seekers.

Paul E. Blackwood
Specialist for Elementary Science
U. S. Department of Health, Education and Welfare
Washington, D. C.

Library of Congress Catalog Card Number: 61-12934

Contents

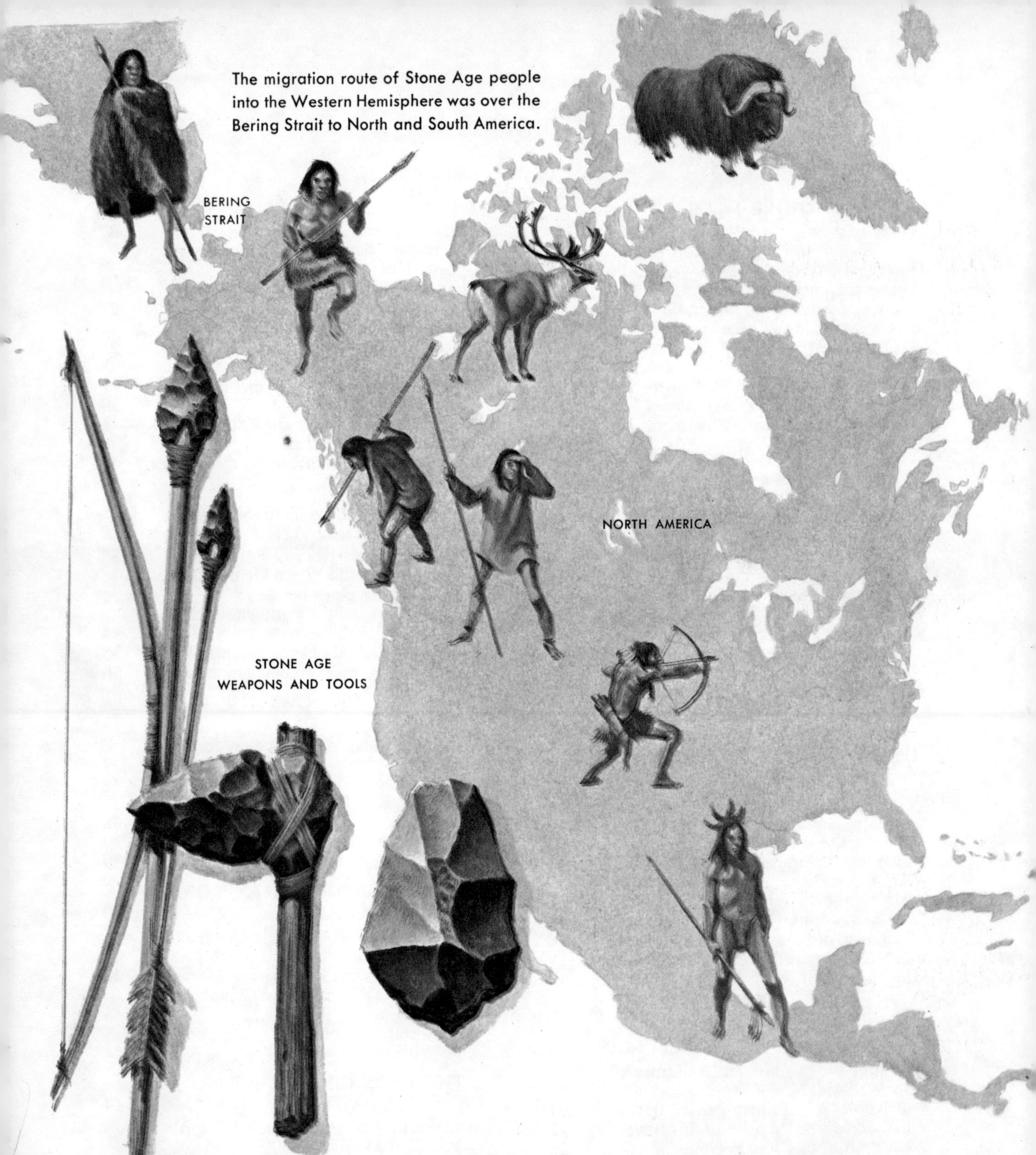

The migration route of Stone Age people into the Western Hemisphere was over the Bering Strait to North and South America.

BERING
STRAIT

STONE AGE
WEAPONS AND TOOLS

NORTH AMERICA

When the Whole World Was New

At the dawn of human history there was a whole world to be discovered. The earth wheeled majestically around the sun, the seasons came and went, and the new race of human beings flexed its muscles and applied its superior brain

to the task of finding food. The search for food was, at that time, the most important and urgent job in the world. In various corners of Europe and Asia small groups of people followed the movements of animal herds, pausing

4

The early inhabitants of the Americas were migratory hunters and fishermen.

SOUTH AMERICA

now and then to sample bits of vegetation. They invented weapons of stone, wood and bone, and with these managed to secure enough food to take care of the tiny traveling communities.

For tens of thousands of years the human race consisted of these small units of migrant hunters who slowly managed to spread over most of the world. The two American continents were settled by such tribes that wandered over the Bering Straits during a period of twenty thousand years. These were Stone Age people who started their migration from the frozen tundras of Siberia and walked through Alaska into the warmer climates of North and South America. All along the way smaller groups remained in places that seemed favorable.

How was the world populated?

5

There, for tens of thousands of years, they were migrant hunters like their relatives in Europe and Asia.

Another form of food gathering is fishing and those people **How were the islands of the world settled?** who reached the shores of the oceans designed primitive boats and went out to spear and net fish. As they improved the boats, the

The Mesopotamian riverboats of 4000 B.C. were small.

The Egyptians used wind-powered boats about the year 6000 B.C. Side oars were used to steer the vessel.

early fishermen were able to sail greater distances. Some were caught in storms and blown far out to sea. Those who survived sometimes landed on strange, uninhabited shores. But many groups never returned, unable to sail against prevailing winds, and started settlements in these new places. It is believed that this is how the islands of the Pacific came to be populated. The same theory may hold true for the British Isles, with the bearded Picts and Celts driving their wood and skin boats across the English

Channel and the North Sea from the great mass of Europe itself.

And so, in the search for food, most of the world came to be populated by the driving, energetic human race.

We cannot call this spread of peoples exploration. Discovery, **What is the purpose of exploration?** yes, because these tribes found most of the areas of the world, but not deliberate exploration. Such exploration comes as the result of a need beyond that of food — a need for other material things, a need for greater room for an expanding population, a need for people to set up religious, social and political systems of their own. Sometimes it is just a need to assemble more knowledge about the far-reaching seas and distant horizons of this home of the human race.

Exploration also implies the setting up of colonies, trade routes and regular exchange between different cultures. Discovery, especially in the primitive ages, was by accident, but exploration has always had a purpose.

There are no dates, but exploration became a function of the human race when it settled down, and the settling down was the result of the invention of agriculture. This took place roughly some ten thousand years ago. When people could raise their food in the same place year after year, they built villages and then cities. All through the Middle East, India, China, and Malay Peninsula and Northern Africa, cities were being erected near the fertile fields.

When was the start of exploration?

And so in the many centuries before the birth of Christ, the human race began to become city and farm dwellers. The nomadic life began to fade as specialized trades developed and money replaced the barter system as a medium of exchange. People became dependent on one another in a way that had never existed before. Some raised food, others made tools, but a very special group still wandered and carved new pathways over the world. They were the explorers.

With most of the population of the world settled, it was the explorers who discovered the routes and set up the commer-

Why were explorers necessary to society?

cial exchanges between different areas. These exchanges were now necessary. Each area of the world was rich in something that the other areas did not possess in the same quantity. It was sometimes a raw material or a manufactured item, like a tool or pottery, or even an ornament that was commonplace in one area, but quite rare and valuable in another. When the people realized the value of these items and felt the need for things they did not have, they set up industries and arranged for sale and trade to the rest of the world. It was the explorers who paved the way for this exchange.

By the year 1000 B.C., trade routes were well set up between all parts of the inhabited world and various goods were shipped back and forth along the roads and sea lanes. Salt and amber came from northern Europe along a road that flanked the great Danube River and then crossed the Alps. Along this path,

What products were exchanged in early days?

Wind and oars powered Greek war galleys in 500 B.C.

too, came the loads of furs and leather heading south to the Mediterranean. But passing these caravans as they toiled steadily toward the sun were caravans moving north. Ivory and glass from Egypt, beautifully carved and tinted, shipped across the water in Phoenician or Egyptian freighters and now loaded in crude wagons, went north to repay the fierce Goths for their furs and leather.

Minoan, Cretan and Phoenician oarsmen powered their craft down the Persian Gulf and into the Arabian Sea to

The metals were most important. Gold and silver were prized for ornaments and for money, but bronze meant more to the economy. The unknown metal workers who accidentally discovered that ten percent of tin mixed with ninety percent of copper resulted in a tough, yet malleable, metal had made a contribution of tremendous value. This metal, bronze, was used for weapons, fittings, bowls, jars — anything where durability was required.

Why was this period called the Bronze Age?

return with loads of spices and incense from Hadramat, the incense center of this early civilization. From the Far East, through the Khyber Pass from India and the well-trodden paths that flanked the Black Sea, came silks, spices and aromatic woods.

Battles were won by countries that first had bronze and they held sway until iron was discovered.

The ingredients for bronze first came from Spain and Hungary. Later, tin was discovered in Great Britain and it arrived in the smelting pots of Crete and

The Phoenician cargo ships sailed to the islands of Britain for tin, to western Africa for spices, to Greece for wine and olives, and to nearby Egypt for linen and grain.

The Goths crossed the Alps with salt and amber packs.

From the trading centers of the Far East came rich caravans with silks, spices and aromatic woods.

Cargo from many ports arrived by boat on the coast of Egypt where it was then unloaded and carried by porters to wagons for transport to inland points.

Carthage after a long journey. Floated across the English Channel by the hardy Celts, the metal was transferred to land vehicles and made the difficult European trip all the way to the Mediterranean where once more it put to sea before it reached its destination.

As one can easily see, the ancient world was well traveled. The routes were definite and trade flourished. But some men wondered. They knew the world was much larger than the tiny mapped area known

Why did the explorations continue?

at that time. So exploration went on. It went on for two reasons. The first was economic. The rulers of the various early empires wanted to extend their control, to rule over new lands, to find new products, to establish new markets for their own products. They wanted to sample new luxuries, find new slaves and, above all, dominate as much of the world as possible.

The other reason for exploration was in the minds of the explorers themselves. Although they were financed and directed by the rulers of the countries, deep within their minds was an entirely different motive. It was a motive that drove them to sail uncharted seas, cross dusty deserts, brave icy glaciers and fight for their lives against hostile peoples.

What were the explorers like?

They were seekers after danger. These explorers were not content to live peaceful, safe lives in the cities. They were men who were not happy unless they risked their lives in the search for the unknown. Did the sun really set in the western sea? Did the ocean actually spill off the sharp cliff-like edge of the world? Were there strange and wonderful people in the mountains that touched the sky?

The explorers set sail to the ends of the earth to answer those questions. Some found their answers and returned triumphant. Others gave their lives and never came back. But all of them fulfilled their great desire — to search for the unknown.

The Early Explorers

No one knows who the first men were that could be called explorers. If any records were kept of their pioneering expeditions, they have long since vanished. But it is certain that men did set out to blaze new trails across the face of the earth in the very early days of civilization. It was due to these unknown men that the first land routes and sea lanes were established. Their names have been forgotten in the dust of the ages.

We owe a great debt of gratitude for almost all of the historical knowledge regarding the two or three thousands years preceding the birth of Christ to three men, all ancient Greeks. The most important was Herodotus who lived from 484 to 425 B.C. and is known as the "Father of History." He can be called the first historian, the first man who set out to write a history of

How did we find out about the early explorers?

HERODOTUS

POLYBIUS

STRABO

man's doings. But he was more than a mere scribe. Herodotus also interpreted history. He tried to explain the reasons for — and the motives behind — the events and the great wars that raged across the Mediterranean during the period of the early civilizations.

The next great historian was Polybius who lived from 201 to 120 B.C. Like Herodotus, Polybius was concerned with motives, and again like his predecessor, he was intensely interested in exploration.

Polybius was followed by Strabo, born in 63 B.C., who tried to make his life work a continuation of the written history of Polybius. But in addition to his writings, Strabo also produced a geography of the world as he knew it.

It was due to the efforts of Herodotus, Polybius and Strabo that today we can know something of the comings and goings of peoples in that far distant age. Because of these three scholarly Greeks,

modern students can share the excitement of the Bronze Age and follow the paths of the early explorers.

Of the explorations that were documented by these historians, three stand out today as significant. They were the voyages of an unnamed Egyptian sea captain, a Carthaginian named Hanno, and Pytheas, a Greek. There were many other expeditions in this period. Some were written about, many others were never recorded, but the three men above were real trail blazers.

Who were some of the important early explorers?

Much of the gold used by the aristocratic Egyptians came from the mouth of the Zambesi River. Egyptian and Phoenician ships often sailed down the eastern coast of Africa, into

What was the Egyptian reason for exploration?

11

the Mozambique Channel, and loaded their holds with the precious metal. The Mozambique Channel runs between the island of Madagascar and the African coast and features a strong southward ocean current. Probably many ships never returned to Egypt, being unable to sail or row against this current, and the Egyptian Pharaoh, Necho II, was determined to find a new route home.

Necho was a powerful ruler, ambitious and imaginative. At one time he attempted to build a canal from the Mediterranean to the Red Sea, on the same site as the present-day Suez Canal! To solve the problem of the Zambesi gold, he equipped a Phoenician fleet with an Egyptian captain and gave him orders to follow the coastline of Africa until he reached the Straits of Gibraltar and returned to Egypt through the Mediterranean. Somehow, somewhere, Necho must have learned that Africa was surrounded by water, but at that time, 600 B.C., the idea of such a voyage was a daring thought.

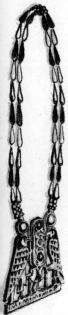

Necho's sea captain set sail. He was

How long did Necho's sea voyage take? away a long time and all hope for his return must have faded, but all Egypt was stirred by excitement when the fleet finally returned — three years later. It was not only the return that was exciting but the fact that the ships came back to Egypt from the west, through the Mediterranean, after having traveled over nine thousand miles completely around Africa! The sea captain proved Necho's theory by this feat, one of the most important of any voyage of discovery.

EGYPTIAN JEWELRY

What was the route taken by Necho's ships? From the Red Sea, into the Indian Ocean, and due south down the coast the tiny fleet rowed and sailed until they reached the southern tip of Africa. Then, turning west, they rounded the base of the continent. Passing the Cape of Good Hope the ships turned north, passing strange lands, seeing strange peoples, desperately clinging to the coast as the mysterious, swelling Atlantic stretched far away to the west. With the passage through the Straits of Gibraltar the pioneering fleet arrived in familiar waters and sailed home triumphantly. Although Pharaoh Necho II had the basic idea and financed the expedition and is now credited as the first man to say that Africa was surrounded by water, the name of the daring sea captain who carried out this dangerous mission remains forever unknown.

Although the story of this adventure was written by Herodotus one hundred fifty years later, the world soon forgot about it. Until 1487, people believed that Africa was connected with Asia and that the Indian Ocean was an inland sea. Three reasons may explain this loss of knowledge — the overland trade routes became better established, gold was discovered nearer the Mediterranean, and the general illiteracy of the early world. There were not many who could read Herodotus.

The routes taken by Necho's sea captain (brown line), Hanno (green line), and Pytheas (red line): Necho's voyage proved that Africa was surrounded by water. Hanno discovered new lands and set up colonies along the northwestern and western coasts of Africa. Pytheas' trip aided science and geography.

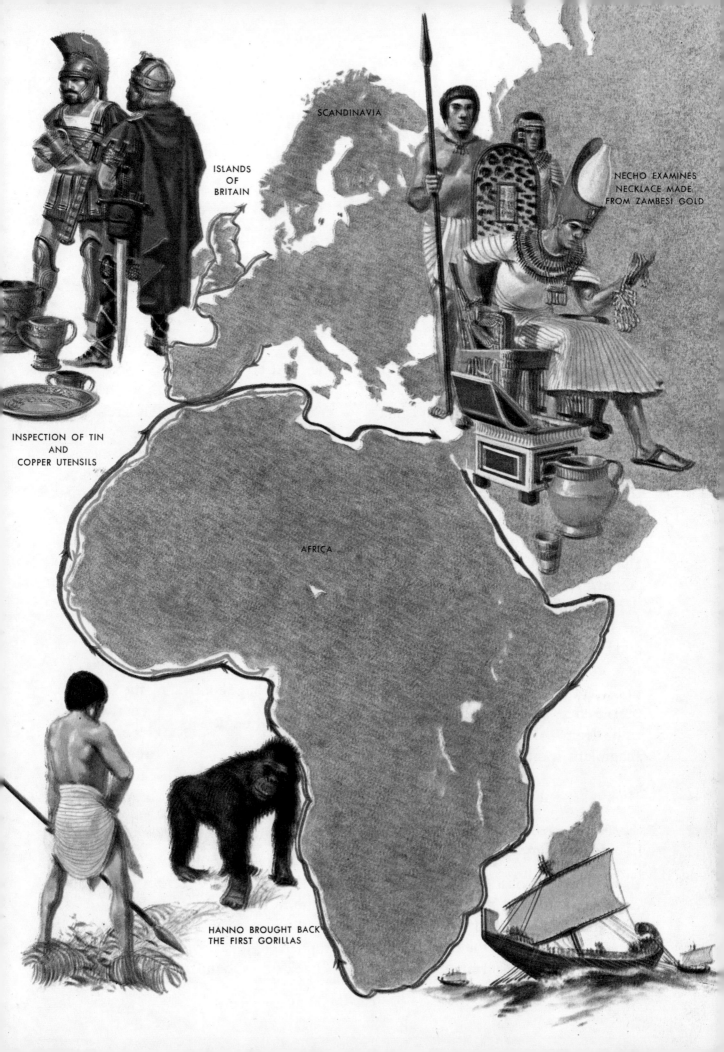

INSPECTION OF TIN
AND
COPPER UTENSILS

ISLANDS
OF
BRITAIN

SCANDINAVIA

NECHO EXAMINES
NECKLACE MADE
FROM ZAMBESI GOLD

AFRICA

HANNO BROUGHT BACK
THE FIRST GORILLAS

About 630 B.C. the Carthaginians began

What were the reasons for the voyages of the Carthaginians? a conquest of the world as they knew it. Great sailors and rugged fighters, they soon dominated the lands bordering on the Mediterranean. Taking control of Spain and North Africa, they straddled the Straits of Gibraltar, or the Pillars of Hercules as they were known then, and exacted toll from all ships. They had economic reasons for this. Tin came from Great Britain by a long, slow overland route, and the Carthaginians wanted a direct and exclusive sea lane to the northern islands. They dispatched Himilco with a huge fleet to Great Britain. He set up an exchange system, and with control of the sea lane, the Carthaginians soon had a monopoly of the tin supply.

The Carthaginian expedition of Hanno in 500 B.C. was a true voyage of colonization, complete with army, settlers and supplies. Fishermen and traders had discovered the Canary Islands and the island of Madeira which are situated off the northwest coast of Africa in the Atlantic Ocean. A highly valued purple dye, extracted from shellfish, came from these islands and the Carthaginians wanted that market also.

Hanno set out with sixty galleys carrying three thousand

What sea route did Hanno take? people and set up colonies all along the northwest coast of Africa. These colonies controlled and protected the sea lanes to the valued islands and insured a monopoly of the dye known as Tyrian purple. But Hanno went far-

ther. After leaving the colonists, he sailed south, as far south as the Cameroons, which is completely around the huge western bulge of the continent. There he discovered Mount Cameroon, the only active volcano in western Africa, and returned with the first gorillas that civilized human beings had ever seen. Hanno would undoubtedly have traveled farther south, but his supplies ran out. That Carthaginian expedition was perhaps the first in the complete tradition of exploration to discover new lands and set up colonies.

With Carthage controlling the sea lanes, their rivals, the

Why did the Greeks explore northward? Greeks, were faced with a difficult problem. Unable to sail out of the Mediterranean, their only trade with the north was through the overland routes — a slow, dangerous process. They needed more information about the northern territories and a sea route to the source of amber.

In 325 B.C., an astronomer and geographer, Pytheas, was selected by the Greek rulers to make the hazardous trip

Pytheas was the first Mediterranean seaman to see the frozen sea. He described it as resembling jellyfish.

various geographic positions. A remarkable man, perhaps the first of the true navigators!

Pytheas sailed to Great Britain, visited Ireland, the Shetland Islands and, in a magnificent six-day voyage across the stormy North Sea, reached northern Norway — the legendary *ultima Thule* of the ancient Greeks, regarded as the farthest part of the habitable world. He was the first man from the south to see the icebound Arctic Ocean and the strange effect of the midnight sun. Then, from Norway, Pytheas sailed south to Germany, the first man to reach that land by water. His return journey to Massilia was overland by an established trade route.

Which lands did Pytheas reach?

to the north. Pytheas lived in Massilia, the ancient site of present-day Marseilles, France. Despite the blockade of the Straits of Gibraltar by the Carthaginians, Pytheas sailed past them and traveled north along the French coast. After going around England, he went north again along the coasts of Holland and Germany.

Pytheas was not an aimless hit-or-miss explorer content to follow a coastline and let chance dictate his destination. He was a scientist. His observation of the stars had led him to believe that a course which followed a fixed star would be accurate, and he carefully selected a group of such stars that surrounded true north. This, hundreds of years before compass or sextant!

What special knowledge did Pytheas use?

He had also calculated tidal movements and in those early days knew that the position of the moon affected the movement of the ocean waters. In addition, he had worked out a system for determining latitudes north of the Equator by timing the length of the day at

Pytheas' contribution to the knowledge of the Bronze Age was immense. He expanded the concept of the world. His establishment of scientific latitude markings gave people a sense of the relative positions of the land masses and their place on the earth. But in addition to geographic discoveries, Pytheas brought back information about the production of amber, the mining of tin and knowledge about the life and customs of the fierce, rugged northern people. He also returned with two new beverages from Great Britain — a primitive beer and mead, a drink made of fermented honey. This mild-mannered scholar, scientist and student of the heavens, opened the door to a newly expanded world.

What did mankind learn from the voyage of Pytheas?

15

Vikings landed in eastern North America.

The Vikings Sail West

When the Roman Empire dominated the world, the period of exciting exploration came temporarily to an end. To be sure, adventurous men still roamed the sea lanes and overland trade routes, but the Romans officially sponsored very few expeditions. They were business men, more interested in expanding their existing trade relations than founding new ones. The Roman emperors strengthened their contacts between remote parts of the world, established a system of monetary exchange and ruled the world with efficiency and brutality. With the fall of the Roman Empire and its tight web of communication between areas, the society of man entered the Dark Ages.

The traders, soldiers and wandering minstrels maintained contact between different areas, but it seemed as though the adventurous spirit of the human race had died. Feudal societies kept a tight grip on the people, cultural exchange ceased and only the scholarly monks of the Catholic Church kept vigil over the accumulation of

Was there contact between countries in the Dark Ages?

16

human knowledge. In their monasteries they preserved the art, literature and music of the human race, while outside their walls petty tyrants and self-declared kings dominated the world.

In the northlands a hardy, independent race of men still roamed the sea lanes.

Was there exploration during the Dark Ages?

They were the Vikings. Brawny, boisterous, valiant fighters, skilled sailors, these blond- and red-bearded Norsemen knew no master. They were the terror of northern Europe, men who welcomed danger and sailed unafraid into strange waters. For over five thousand years the Viking ships had traveled the oceans of the world. It is believed that they visited every sea known to the men of the Bronze Age.

Basically the Vikings were neither traders nor merchants. They explored in order to colonize. A pastoral people, herding cattle, growing crops and fishing the sea, they sought to expand their living space. This may sound peaceful, but it was not. The Vikings were ruthless invaders and the gentler peoples of the Mediterranean were lucky that these masters of the icy seas of the north did not attempt to colonize the sun-warmed southlands.

What did the Vikings seek?

The secret of the Viking success against the smashing waves of the northern oceans lay in their ships. Probably designed back in the late Stone Age period, these ships were sleek and fast.

What kind of ships did the Vikings use?

From their home in the northlands, the ruthless Vikings raided Scotland and Ireland. They also discovered Iceland and Greenland, and landed on the American continent before Columbus did. Their two most daring voyages: those of Eric the Red (broken line) and Leif Ericsson (solid line).

GREENLAND
SCANDINAVIA
ICELAND
SCOTLAND
IRELAND
NORTH AMERICA

Some eighty feet long, sixteen feet wide, they featured a stubby mast with a large square sail. The main driving power was supplied by oarsmen, sixteen to a side. This combination gave the Viking ships a great advantage in battle. The slender keel and long oaken planks allowed the vessels to withstand the pounding of huge waves. Compared with the Egyptian and Grecian galleys, they must have looked like thoroughbreds in the company of plow horses.

It was these ships that carried the Vikings to North America hundreds of years before Columbus was born. The daring Norsemen were the first to visit the New World and bring back news of a wonderful and interesting land.

To get to North America, the Vikings used a series of island stepping-stones, settling on each one and establishing a thriving colony. Sailing their dragon-crested ships toward the setting

Which land did the Vikings first explore?

sun, they first arrived at Iceland in the year A.D. 863. But to their great surprise, the island was inhabited! An order of Irish monks had come there some fifty years earlier looking for a quiet place to set up a hermitage and pursue their worship in peace. Their peace was not long-lived. The pagan Norsemen ruthlessly eliminated the peaceful monks. Iceland became a well established colony to which many Norsemen came to build a new life.

One of the groups that migrated there in the following century was the Asvaldsson family, which included a tough, quarrelsome, red-haired boy named Eric. He came by his fighting nature quite honestly. Eric's grandfather was a notorious troublemaker back in Norway, and his father had been banished to Iceland for killing a man. When Eric grew up, he became involved in quarrels and was twice responsible for killing his countrymen. The authorities punished him with three years of banishment, never dreaming

Irish monks actually landed in Iceland before the Vikings, but they were eliminated by the Viking bands.

18

that this sentence would result in the eventual discovery of the New World.

Eric the Red gathered his family and

What discovery did Eric the Red make?

servants and set sail to the west in the year 982. On that voyage he discovered Greenland. He spent the rest of his exile in exploring the many small islands in the area and when the three years were ended he returned to Iceland. There he immediately equipped an expedition of over seven hundred people and twenty-five ships. These people became the original colonizers of Greenland. The fierce Eric the Red ruled over them as a self-appointed king.

The next step in the spread of the Vikings was to the mainland of North America itself.

By the year 1000, Leif Ericsson, son of

Who discovered North America?

Eric the Red, was old enough to continue the exploring tradition of his father. Leif became the first to set foot on North America. His expedition consisted of a single ship manned by thirty-five Vikings. The ship itself had a tradition. It was purchased from Bjarni Herjulfsson, a Viking explorer who may or may not have discovered America before Leif. Herjulfsson made his voyage in 985, but the written account of his trip and the places he claimed to have visited do not seem to be accurate. Most historians do not accept his claims. There is, however, little doubt that Leif Ericsson did land in North America.

He called the land of his discovery "Vinland the Fair." Vinland means Wineland and presumably Leif referred to the great number of wild grapes he found growing along the eastern coastline. He described and mapped areas that many people recognize today as Cape Cod, Massachusetts and the is-

Eric the Red, a self-appointed king, ruled Greenland.

lands of Nantucket and Martha's Vineyard. Historians have made many claims about the possible landing sites of the Vikings, which include Newfoundland, Nova Scotia, Maine, Massachusetts and Virginia to name a few, but the true identity of Leif Ericsson's Vinland has never been accurately established.

Leif Ericsson returned to Greenland a year later with the news of his discovery. It was a great voyage and one of the most important in man's history.

Why did Viking colonies fail in North America?

It was only natural that attempts at colonization should follow Leif's epic voyage, and in the year 1003, a small fleet sailed to North America. It was captained by Thorfinn Karselfni, a merchant and trader. He brought three ships loaded with men and their families, and even domestic animals. The expedition settled somewhere along the eastern coast and began to farm the land. But they were attacked time and time again by Indian tribes. The *skraelings,* as the Norsemen called the Indians, were too many even for the fierce Viking warriors. Outnumbered as they were, it was a losing battle, and finally in 1006 one lone ship returned to Greenland with the survivors.

North America was abandoned by the Norsemen and the continent had to wait until the Middle Ages and the voyage of Columbus to be rediscovered.

The Long Walk of Marco Polo

Very slowly the world began to awaken. It was now a different world. The Mohammedans controlled the Near East and the Mongol Empire stretched all the way from the Pacific to the Black Sea. The trade routes were still in use, but heavy tribute had to be paid to almost every local king along the way. Rich luxuries occasionally came from China and India, spices, perfume, silk, wood, exotic foods, but it was a long, slow process. In 1095, Pope Urban declared the start of the Holy Crusades to the East, in order to open the way for pilgrimages to the birthplace of Christ. But the economic reason for the Crusades was also important. The Europeans wanted to develop a free trade with the Far East. Spices were very necessary to help preserve food in those days, and the demand for silk was great.

The Crusades not only opened more of the trade routes, but still further increased the desire of Europeans for Eastern goods. The independent city of Venice became the sea ruler of the Mediterranean, sending her ships to the Near

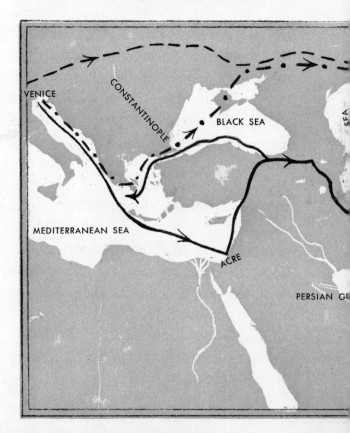

East in regular convoys, and Venetian merchants soon established land caravans all the way to China. The world was indeed awakening.

In the year 1260, two brothers made the trip to Peking, China, where they met Kublai Khan, the absolute ruler of the Mongol Empire. Their names were Nicolo and Maffeo Polo, successful Venetian merchants. They had made many business trips to the East, but this journey had an extremely important result. Kublai Khan had become interested in Christianity! Strangely enough, this powerful man feared his own pagan religious leaders whom he called idolaters. He wanted the Polo brothers to go back to Europe and return with one hundred Christian monks who, by reason of their education, could confuse and out-argue his idolaters. Then he would pub-

Who were the two brothers who traveled to old China?

licly denounce them and have them executed. Should this plan succeed, Kublai Khan promised to convert the entire Mongol Empire to Christianity!

The Polo brothers traveled the long dusty route back to Europe and brought the Khan's message to the Pope. Pope Gregory X then assigned two monks (no more could be spared) to travel with the party all the way to China. Both deserted before Armenia had been crossed and the Khan was never able to carry out his plan for converting the Mongol Empire.

But the trip was not a loss, even with the failure of the mission. The party

Was Kublai Khan's plan carried out?

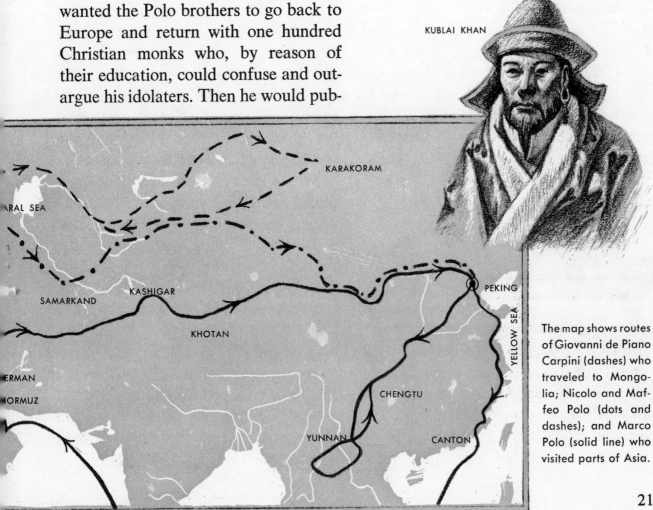

KUBLAI KHAN

The map shows routes of Giovanni de Piano Carpini (dashes) who traveled to Mongolia; Nicolo and Maffeo Polo (dots and dashes); and Marco Polo (solid line) who visited parts of Asia.

21

MARCO POLO

With tablets of "safe conduct" like the ones illustrated, the Polo brothers traveled un-molested through Asia.

included an intelligent, sensitive teen-ager — Marco, the son of Maffeo Polo. His report of the travels through the East and his descriptions of the culture and customs he saw did a great deal to change future history.

The Polo family sailed from Venice to Acre in the Middle East, in the year 1271. Their original intention was to cross to the Red Sea and sail down to the Indian Ocean and reach China by water, but for some, now unknown, reason this plan was abandoned. They turned north, walked through Persia, then east into the Mongol Empire.

Marco wrote of the crossing of the Pamir Pla-teau, an ex-tremely high, arid region with intense cold. He noted the lack of oxygen by observing that fires burned slowly and water boiled at a lower temperature than usual. From Pamir they crossed the Gobi Des-ert where they were beset by supersti-tious fears about monsters that were

What did Marco Polo see on his travels?

supposed to roam the sands. But the Venetians pushed on into the steppes of Mongolia. Marco was the first to tell of the Tartars, a truly nomadic people who wandered over the land in the fash-ion of the Stone Age hunters. These migrant tribes carried their homes with them — small compact *yurts,* or tents, made of hand-pounded felt. With these tents packed on the sturdy Mongolian ponies, the Tartars were free to wander, driving their animals with them.

Finally, Marco Polo came to the Great Wall of China, one of the won-ders of the world. It was built some 2,200 years ago and is over 1,400 miles in length. The ancient emperors of China erected this magnificent wall to guard their domain against the Mongols to the north. The massive stone struc-ture is wide enough to have a road along the top, with defensive forts at spaced intervals. It runs through deserts and crosses rugged mountains, streams and quiet farmlands. Even today, the sight of this wall stretching across lonely Mongolia is a testament to the energy of the human race.

With the crossing of Mongolia com-pleted, the Polo family reached Kublai Khan's summer capital at Shangtu, and accompanied him to Peking, his winter capital. It was the year 1275, and the long walk had taken four years.

Peking is one of the oldest cities of China. It was famous even in the earli-est times of civilization. Legends came to the western world about the beauty, the luxury, the wonders of this ancient capital, but it was not until Marco Polo wrote of its marvels that the world had a first-hand account of the city.

Peking was first built in the twelfth century B.C. and was called Ch'i.

What kind of city was Peking, China?

The Oriental dynasties kept renaming it every time a new group took power. It was renamed Yen, Yu-Chow, Nan Chung and Changtu under the ancient Khans. When Kublai Khan rose to power he made it his capital and called it Cambaluc or *Kaanbalig*—City of the Khan. After Kublai, the Ming dynasties named it Peiping-Fu and then Peking. In our time it has been renamed Peiping, but most people still say Peking.

Cambaluc — ancient Peking — to which the young Marco Polo came, was a city of wonders. It was surrounded by a huge stone wall, fifty feet high and fifteen feet wide. Within the city was an inner city, also walled, which contained the court and retinue of the Khan. All through Cambaluc stood tall, many-tiered pagodas trimmed in porcelain with gilded roofs shining in the sun. The famous, massive drum tower was erected by Kublai Khan and long broad streets crossed the city in regular rows. It was a place of luxury for those who were fortunate enough to belong to the aristocracy and a place of slavery and toil for those who served the masters.

When Marco Polo met the great Kublai Khan, he so impressed the ruler with his intelligence that Marco became his private secretary. But the young Venetian was also impressed by his employer. Kublai Khan was a cultured man and a fine administrator. He had divided the empire into provinces, each ruled by a governor. From province to province he

What kind of man was Kublai Khan?

The brothers Nicolo and Maffeo Polo, Venetian merchants, made the long trip to fabled China and back to Europe.

Venice: Marco Polo's day

had designed roads that were long, straight and tree-lined, and along these highways an efficient mail and messenger service operated. The Khan was a kind and generous man, often helping starving areas with food stored in government stockpiles. He supported artists, musicians, writers, and in almost every way was a benevolent ruler. But there was another side to his character. In war and politics he was ruthless. Kublai Khan conquered and annexed every area he possibly could and disposed of his enemies with vicious savagery. In a way, he was like the eternal Oriental symbol, the Yin and Yang, which represents both good and evil.

In the service of the Khan, Marco Polo was required to travel extensively throughout China. He visited the lofty plateau of Tibet, the long seacoast, and even went into Burma. He heard of the wondrous land of Chipangu, as Japan was then known — the land of golden temples. He heard the strange music,

learned the Chinese method of astronomical observation and saw gunpowder used effectively in artillery pieces. Finally, he was made governor of Manzi province and lived in its capital city.

The Polo family became rich and influential during their stay in China. But **Why did Marco Polo finally leave China?** fearing for their lives should the Khan die, they made plans to return to their homeland. Fortunately a mission was available. The Khan of Persia had requested a Mongol bride and the Polo family accepted the task of delivering the young lady to her new home. This time they traveled by sea, taking a Chinese junk down the coast and around the Malay Peninsula to India. After visiting Ceylon and several coastal cities in India, the party sailed to Ormuz and then walked to Tabriz in Persia, where they delivered the new bride.

From Tabriz the route was familiar

24

Peking: Marco Polo's day

— overland to the Black Sea, by ship past Constantinople into the friendly Mediterranean and home to Venice. The year was 1295 and Marco Polo had been gone for twenty-four years. The seventeen-year-old youth returned as a mature man of forty-one, his mind full of the wonders he had seen.

Marco Polo wrote a huge book of his experiences, recounting everything in detail. The Europeans were overwhelmed by the tales he told, but also felt that he had exaggerated. We know now that Marco Polo told the truth, but to the people of his time the glittering descriptions of Oriental life and customs seemed overdrawn. Although he was ridiculed, his book made a great impression, for it stimulated a great interest in the Orient. The Europeans wanted to sample the exotic foods, dress in the silky fabrics and util-

What happened as a result of Marco Polo's writings?

ize the scientific and military instruments. A great drive to the East was started, with many caravans toiling along the roads to China and India. Navigators began plotting possible sea routes to the fabled lands that Marco Polo described and the entire Western world began to look to the East.

Marco Polo cannot be called an explorer in the sense that he went to search for unknown lands or colonize new territories, but he was an explorer in the sense that he opened men's minds to new cultural ideas and stimulated new contacts between different countries. The long walk of Marco Polo started a trend that led to the great age of exploration.

25

Columbus left Palos, Spain on August 3, 1492 in his flagship *Santa Maria* (foreground), followed by the *Nina* and *Pinta*.

Columbus and the Rediscovery of America

By the fifteenth century the Western world was in earnest about finding a sea route to the Far East. It was the age-old problem — not enough goods were arriving from the faraway lands. This time it was due to two powerful groups. The Turks had become extremely powerful and managed to blockade many of the overland caravans, while the Arabians controlled the waters of the eastern Mediterranean and the Red Sea. It seemed as though every time a new contact was established with the Orient, some nation turned up to block further exchange. So once more the explorers went forth.

In the fifteenth century most people had

Was Columbus the only person who believed that the earth was round?

forgotten that it was possible to sail around Africa. A notion had been growing for a long time that China, India and the East Indies could be reached by sailing westward across the Atlantic. The notion was correct, but no one knew that two mighty continents — almost stretching from pole to pole — blocked the way. They were the Americas.

To believe that one could sail to the East by sailing west, one must also believe that the earth is a sphere. A Genoese sea captain named Christopher Columbus believed this, but he was not alone. He was not alone by many centuries, for as far back as 500 B.C., a Greek scholar, Pythagoras, asserted that the earth was round. A Norwegian textbook written in 1250 not only said the same thing, but also gave the reasons for the varying climates of the earth, the angle of the sun at different times of the year and the prevailing winds. Not all the ancient knowledge had been lost — it was just out of favor for a while.

Columbus seemed to have dedicated his life to just one purpose — that of making a trip across the Atlantic to the East Indies. He studied astronomy, map making, navigation, and even sailed to England and Iceland where he heard about the Viking voyages. He did, however, make a great mistake. He assumed the world to be much smaller than it really was, and he thought that Asia was much larger than we know it to be. But he was determined to make the voyage. Columbus had a mission, not for any country or monarch, but for himself.

Why did Columbus want to sail to the East Indies?

Columbus first went to Portugal to King John II. The Portuguese were the master mariners of the age and he felt that they would surely back his plan. However, the Portuguese king had a plan of his own, to send a fleet around Africa to India. The scheme of Columbus seemed impractical. It meant sailing out of sight of land for many weeks in an unexplored ocean. Columbus was turned down and he left Portugal in 1484.

Where did Columbus get the money for his historic trip?

He went to Spain hoping to get financial backing for his expedition from Queen Isabella. Just as in Portugal, his plan was received with disfavor. There were conflicting viewpoints and much court intrigue in Spain, so Columbus sent his brother Bartholomew to England to gain the interest of Henry VII. Time passed and the landbound sailor grew impatient. It seemed as though his great mission would never be fulfilled. In January, 1492, he started for France, but at the same time his friends at the Spanish court had finally convinced Queen Isabella that if Columbus should succeed, Spain would become rich and powerful. Isabella decided to back the expedition, even with her personal fortune, and Columbus was recalled. On April 17, 1492, both the queen and the captain from Genoa signed a contract for the voyage.

On August 3, 1492, Columbus boarded his flagship, the *Santa Maria*, and consulted his maps. In the harbor of Palos the caravels *Nina* and *Pinta* also heaved gently in the ocean swell. The sails were unfurled and the three ships stood out to sea. Ahead loomed the limitless Atlantic and in the minds of the crew loomed dread fear. The old stories of sea monsters cropped up in addition to the fear of howling storms and thunderous waves. But their captain urged them on. Over eighty men and three small ships started out that morning and sailed into history.

How many men and ships set sail with Columbus?

Columbus was equipped with the

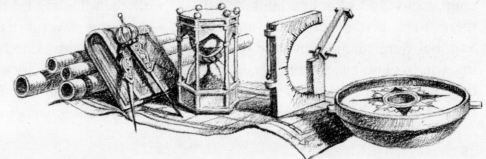

Columbus had a compass, quadrant, dividers and an hourglass timepiece to help him guide his fleet across the sea.

best navigational equipment of his time — compass, dividers, quadrant, sand glass and the best maps available. The most important map was drawn by an Italian physician and astronomer, Toscanelli, and it showed the world to be round. With the aid of this map and a good knowledge of the position of the fixed stars, Columbus was able to set his course due west and head for what he thought was Asia.

After a stop at the Canary Islands, the little fleet sailed into completely unknown waters. From this point on, all happenings were new, even to the most experienced sailors. Their compass needles showed a greater westerly variation, the floating seaweed of the Sargasso Sea was encountered and they even saw a meteorite fall into the ocean. But as August passed, September passed and October came, the Atlantic still stretched before them, a panorama of heaving waves all the way to the horizon. There was no land, only water in every direction.

In the second week of October, a mutiny began to break out among the men, and the

Why did Columbus' captains want to return to Spain?

captains of the *Nina* and the *Pinta* came to Columbus and asked him to turn back. They had good reasons. Neither man was superstitious and each was as courageous as Columbus himself, but there were certain practical matters. Supplies were running low, the prevailing winds blew away from Spain and they wanted to return before they all starved on the limitless ocean. Colum-

bus stood firm. He had spent his whole life preparing for this voyage and he was sure that land was near. This was not guesswork on his part. Migrating birds had been seen overhead and so Columbus bargained for three more days. But his captains set a condition. Should land not be sighted by the evening of October 12, the fleet was to put about for Spain.

The ships continued to the west and on October 11, some branches

Where did Columbus and his crew land?

were seen floating on the surface of the water and several hand-carved poles were fished up. Land did seem to be ahead. At ten o'clock that night, Columbus saw light far ahead, and at two o'clock the following morning, the night

Columbus set foot in the New World on an island he named San Salvador.

The map shows Columbus' voyages. First voyage: 1492-93 (solid line). Second voyage: 1493-96 (dotted line). Third voyage: 1498 (dashes). Last: 1502-04 (dots-dashes).

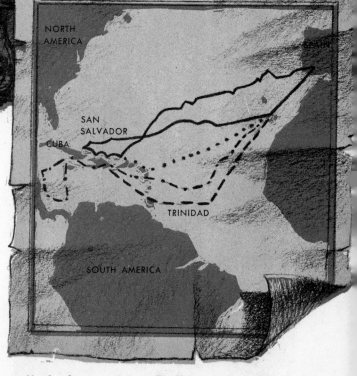

lookout on the *Pinta* sighted land on the horizon. When the sun rose, the little fleet reached an anchorage near an island of the New World and Columbus himself was the first to step ashore. It was almost five hundred years since Leif Ericsson had seen the wooded shores of North America and the continent was now rediscovered. But no one knew that. They all thought Asia had been reached.

Columbus landed on an island which he named San Salvador. Its real name, as spoken by the natives that he met, was Guanahani. Today we know it as Watlings Island, one of the many dots of land that make up the Bahamas. Columbus took possession of this island for Spain and greatly impressed the natives with his rich robes. Believing that he was somewhere in the East Indies, he called the natives Indians, an error which even causes confusion today.

Columbus did some exploring in the Caribbean after he had replenished the supplies of his fleet.

Which other areas in the Americas did Columbus explore?

After discovering many more of the is-

29

Balboa was the first European to look at the Pacific Ocean.

Cortes led his army into Mexico and conquered the Aztecs, ruled by Montezuma.

lands of the Bahama group, he landed in Cuba and then Haiti. The *Santa Maria* was beached on Haiti, due to bad handling, and had to be left there. Columbus took advantage of the incident, built a fort from the wood of the ship, named it *La Navidad* and left forty-four men behind as the basis for a colony. There were no problems with the native inhabitants of the islands who were full of awe for the Europeans. They treated them as guests, never realizing that in coming years their "guests" would prove to be the forerunners of ruthless conquerors.

Columbus returned to Spain on March 15, 1493. It was a triumphant homecoming. He met Queen Isabella at Barcelona and showed her the many exotic items he had collected. Strange birds and animals, cotton, intricate wood carvings and, most interesting of all, several Indians. But he also brought gold. The rulers of Spain saw the opportunity and moved rapidly, sponsoring three more voyages for Columbus. Eventually, he touched on almost every major island in the Caribbean, landed in several places in Central America and discovered South America. He established many colonies, and large quantities of gold and Indian slaves began to arrive in Spain.

Amerigo Vespucci, another Italian sea captain sailing for Spain, reportedly made three voyages to the American continent. Some historians believe that these explorations were limited to the northeastern part of South Amer-

How did the New World get to be called *America*?

Searching for the fabled Fountain of Youth, Juan Ponce de León reached Florida in 1513.

ica, though Vespucci may have made more extensive trips along the west coasts of South and North America, as well as the Caribbean. It was Vespucci who realized that these lands were not part of Asia, but a new land mass that blocked an open sea route to the Orient. His written accounts of the voyages were widely reported throughout Europe, and although Vespucci was not the discoverer of America, the popularity of his writings gave rise to the name of the New World — after the explorer's first name.

Another proof that this really was a New World came on September 26, 1513. Vasco Nuñez de Balboa, a Spanish conqueror and governor of the area that is now Panama, fell out of favor with the Spanish royalty. In an effort to show the crown his value to Spain, he set out on an expedition of discovery across the Isthmus. When he reached the highest ridge of the mountain range, a new and broad ocean stretched far before him. Balboa, at that moment, became the first man in history to see the Pacific Ocean from the west.

There was still a long way to travel before Asia could be reached. The world suddenly proved to be much larger than anyone had ever dreamed.

De Soto, seeking gold, advanced thousands of miles and is credited with discovering the Mississippi.

The Spanish capitalized on the finding of riches in the Americas. Expedition after expedition was sent to the New World. Armies were recruited, local governments were organized and missionaries traveled

How did Spain profit from the discoveries in the Americas?

Pizarro, landing on the west coast of South America, plundered the Inca Empire of Peru.

with the conquerors to convert the Indians. The conquerors, or *conquistadors,* of Spain carried the Spanish flag into many areas of the New World. Juan Ponce de León, governor of Porto Rico, landed in Florida in 1513 and took possession of the entire peninsula. His mission was his own — he was searching for a fountain of miraculous water that could restore one's youth.

Hernando Cortes, a ruthless soldier and mayor of Santiago, Cuba, was sent to Yucatán in Mexico to rescue a Spanish force. He succeeded and then led his army all the way to Mexico City, defeated the Aztec forces of Montezuma and claimed the land for Spain. In 1537, Francisco Pizarro, a member of the Balboa expedition, made his earlier discovery of Peru more secure by defeating the Incas. Two other Spanish warriors went deep into the area of the United States. Fernando de Soto discovered the Mississippi in 1541 and, in the same year, Francisco Coronado led an expedition through the American southwest and up into central Kansas. These cruel but daring men helped strengthen the Spanish claim to the Americas.

Spain became immensely wealthy as gold and other precious minerals of the New World were drained into Spanish galleons and sent to the royal court. The conquest was ruthless and domination of the Indians was barbaric. Spain had no need to search farther. This was not Asia, but it was just as good.

Vasco da Gama — the Second Man Around Africa

PRINCE HENRY THE NAVIGATOR

In 1460 a great man died and another was born. Portugal mourned the death of Prince Henry and no one but his parents applauded the birth of Vasco da Gama. Yet this newborn baby was destined to complete the life work of the prince. The baby could not be aware that his future was fixed in a path determined by one of the most energetic and original thinkers of the fifteenth century.

Who was Prince Henry of Portugal? Prince Henry of Portugal was born in 1394 to the royal family of King John I and Queen Philippa. In his teens he joined his brothers in a war against the Moors and helped capture the port city of Ceuta in North Africa, giving his country control of that age-old gateway, the Straits of Gibraltar. Henry was a burning patriot, determined to make Portugal the foremost nation of the world, but he could never become ruler of his country. Three older brothers had prior rights and the young prince, at the age of twenty, retired to live a monastic life. He selected the little town of Sagres, perched on a rocky point at the extreme southwest tip of Portugal where the swelling waves of the Atlantic crashed in huge breakers against this outpost of the European continent.

The call of the unknown was strong within him. He longed to sail strange seas and discover new lands, but Prince Henry never left Sagres. He has become known as one of the greatest explorers of history, a man who made his country an important maritime and colonial power, a man who today is remembered as "Prince Henry the Navigator."

In the fifteenth century men had forgotten that Africa could be sailed around. They thought that it curved southward in a great sweep and joined India and Asia. But Prince Henry believed that Africa was a separate continent and if a ship could only sail around the southern tip, it would find open water all the way to India. The reason for getting to India by sailing around Africa was classic by that time. The Arabs controlled the Middle East waterways and the world at the time of Prince Henry was looking for another route.

He set up one of the most extraordinary schools of his time. It was a college for seamen, shipbuilders and navigators. There, the best sailors of Portugal

What measures did Prince Henry take to carry out his plans for Africa?

Prince Henry developed the caravel for extended ocean voyages.

were trained by Prince Henry to navigate unknown seas in all types of weather. The men working with him devised new methods of keeping charts, reading the compass and using the astrolabe for determining position. Tables of distances, devices to record speed of travel, every scientific method possible was used by this college to make navigation more predictable.

The crowning glory of all the effort was the design of a new type of ship. The European square-riggers were strong, solidly built vessels, but they were at the mercy of the winds. They had to go where the winds blew or wait until the winds changed. Prince Henry, however, had seen the Arabian dhows in action. They used triangular lateen sails that enabled them to tack and quarter against any wind and make headway. Obviously a combination of both systems, the strength of the European ships and the maneuverability of the Arabian dhows, was the logical answer for extended ocean voyages.

Prince Henry's new ship was called a caravel. It combined the square-rigged sails needed for speed in running downwind with one or two triangular lateen sails for cross-wind sailing. The hull had both strength and sleekness. It was just what was needed to sail southward down the coast of Africa against the turbulent Atlantic and into the teeth of the steady trade wind that blows from the southeast.

Now Prince Henry had his ships, his scientific instruments, his trained navigators — and the great adventure began. His sea captains

What voyages did the Portuguese sea captains make?

Indians in outrigger boats were the first natives seen by da Gama when he anchored off India in 1498.

began to sail into the Atlantic and to the south. It was early in the fifteenth century, but the future of the yet-to-be-born Vasco da Gama was assured. Sailing around the African continent was a long and gradual process. In 1432, the Azores were rediscovered, but the rest of the trips were not as easy. The caravels returned time and time again due to the fears of the sailors. Cape Bojador was one of the landmarks of these voyages. Although it lies only partly around the western bulge of the continent, the sea runs strongly past it —and to the Portuguese captains, great mysteries seemed to lie beyond it. Finally, in 1434, Gil Eannes managed to calm his fears and control his crew and sail boldly on.

Year after year Prince Henry sent his captains out with orders to sail as far south as they dared. And so the long mysterious coast of Africa came slowly back into the knowledge of man. Cape Blanc in 1441, Cape Verde in 1445, and still they sailed to the south. Each man returned to Prince Henry — this landbound genius of explorers — with more information. He added the details to his charts, made calculations and sent the ships out again. The Portuguese court was excited over the success of each expedition. They came to believe that India was within their grasp. Let the Moslems blockade the Mediterranean. Prince Henry's men would find a new way!

Although Prince Henry died in 1460, the Portuguese continued his work and sailed south. The navigational principles were established and the way was open. All that remained was for some-

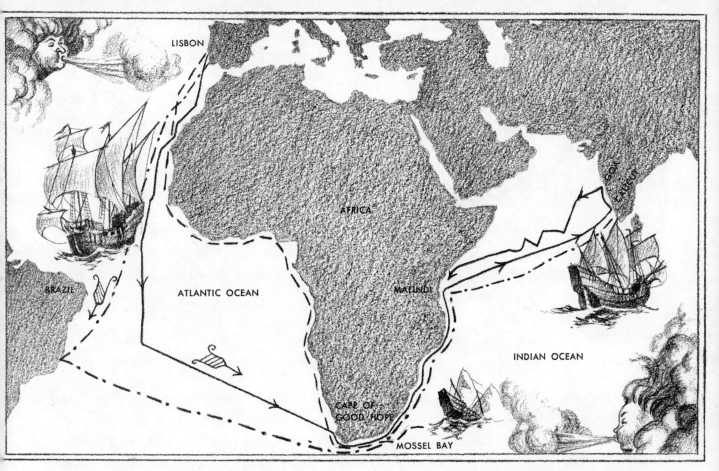

LISBON · AFRICA · BRAZIL · ATLANTIC OCEAN · MATINDI · INDIAN OCEAN · CAPE OF GOOD HOPE · MOSSEL BAY · GOA · CALICUT

The map shows the voyages of Bartholomew Dias (dashes), Vasco da Gama (solid line) and Pedro Alvares Cabral (dots and dashes). Dias was the first European to sail around the Cape of Good Hope (1487-1488). Da Gama was the first European to reach India by a sea route (1498). Cabral sailed around Africa to India (1500-1501), where he set up several colonies for the Portuguese. Dias and da Gama also sailed for Portugal, their homeland.

one to do it. Bartholomew Dias almost made it in 1488. He followed the instructions. Sail south down the coast of Africa, but once past the bulge forsake the coastline and head due south into the open Atlantic. Never mind the fears of the open ocean — avoid the safe coastline — sail south, keep the trade wind on the port bow. Then when the latitude of the Cape of Good Hope is reached, turn east on the new wind that blows from the west. This analysis of the prevailing winds was a master stroke, one of the most important developments from the school of Prince Henry. Dias sailed partly around Africa, to Mossel Bay, but a near mutiny forced him to return to Portugal.

When did Vasco da Gama reach India?

Ten years after Dias' voyage, the man who had been born when Prince Henry died fulfilled the longings of the land-bound navigator and reached India. Vasco da Gama sailed under the orders of King John II, who recognized the ability of this fine seaman. Leaving in July, 1497, he sailed out into the Atlantic, set his course partly to the west and piloted his fleet far to the south. Then, like Dias, he turned east and rounded the tip of Africa. After a landing on the east coast of the continent, da Gama set sail into the rising sun. On May 20, 1498, he landed on the Malabar coast of India. It was done!

Vasco da Gama was warmly received at the royal court in Calicut, a city in southern India on the Malabar Coast.

For centuries men had searched for a water route to the east. Some years earlier Columbus had sailed west and found a new continent, but not Asia. Now Vasco da Gama, the latest in the long line of Portuguese mariners, had found that route.

When da Gama returned, a new expedition was outfitted immediately. The Portuguese were ready to colonize.

Were the Portuguese colonies successful?

Pedro Alvares Cabral left with a fleet of thirteen ships. He arrived in India and set up several colonies. It was specifically due to the voyages of da Gama and Cabral that Portugal gained a vast number of overseas colonies. Some still belong to her, even today.

Behind these glorious exploits looms the brooding figure of a man whose vision and driving purpose conquered the rolling oceans, a man who never left the land and explored with the eyes of others — Prince Henry the Navigator.

John Cabot Follows the Path of the Vikings

In the Moslem city of Mecca a merchant born in Genoa had a brilliant idea. All the wonderful goods and spices of the East were for sale in that teeming city, but no European could buy them directly from the source. The Mos-

lems acted as middlemen, making a tidy profit on each transaction. The merchant, who was also a master mariner, decided to get to the Far East by sailing around the world.

He left Mecca, his brain spinning

with plans. He knew where to get a ship, what route to follow and how to finance the expedition. This merchant was named Giovanni Caboto, a name he shortened to John Cabot when he went to England.

In England, Cabot went to the leading merchants rather than the royal family. As a merchant himself, he knew how to appeal to business men. Although the crown might desire prestige, he felt sure that the English business men would be more certain to back

Where did Cabot get the money for his voyage?

his venture. They did, and with great haste. It had just been learned that Columbus had sailed to the Indies. They did not want the Spanish merchants to control the trade routes, and the British monarch, Henry VII, did not relish the prospect of a Spanish empire.

All parties combined to hurry Cabot on his way. His ship *Mathew* was outfitted by the merchants and the king gave him authority to take all lands in the name of England. And so, on May 2, 1497, John Cabot assembled his crew of eighteen men and set out to sea from Bristol, England. He was heading west to Asia.

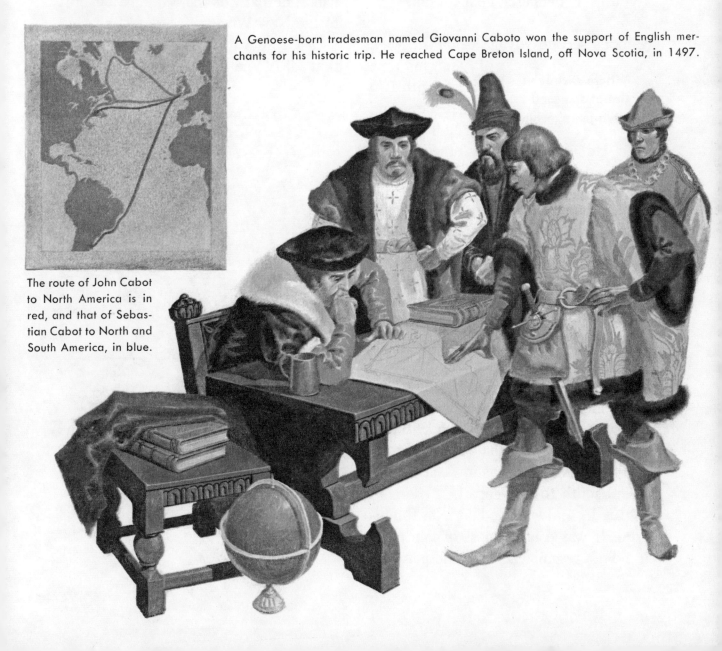

A Genoese-born tradesman named Giovanni Caboto won the support of English merchants for his historic trip. He reached Cape Breton Island, off Nova Scotia, in 1497.

The route of John Cabot to North America is in red, and that of Sebastian Cabot to North and South America, in blue.

Cabot knew of the voyage of Leif Erics-son. He was sure that Leif had landed in northern

What route did Cabot follow?

Asia and that it must be close to Europe at that point. Therefore, he set a course across the North Atlantic, the old path of the Vikings.

Cabot landed at Cape Breton Island on June 24, 1497, claimed it for King Henry VII, then turned north up the coastline, naming all the islands on the way. He was sure that this was northern Asia, and with dreams of the riches of the East, he turned back to England to outfit a commercial expedition.

Cabot's second voyage began in May, 1498. This time he left with two large ships and three hundred

Where did John Cabot's second voyage take him?

men. He intended to reach the shore of Asia and sail south until he came to the fabled islands of Japan. For this journey even King Henry VII had contributed money. This voyage was faster than the first, with the first stop at Greenland, which Cabot thought to be part of the mainland of Asia. Then came a series of heartbreaking disappointments. After sailing up both the eastern and western coasts of Greenland, it became apparent that it was just an island. Once more Cabot pointed his ships to the west. This time they made Baffin Land, well within the Arctic Circle. Again thinking he was in Asia, Cabot sailed south to find Japan.

But he only arrived at Newfoundland. It was a large mass of land, but it did not resemble Asia. In desperation he urged his ships farther to the south. They passed through the area he had explored on his first voyage and went on down the coast of North America. No one knows how far they traveled.

Some say that John Cabot may have sailed as far south as Florida, the holds of his ships filled with goods for trade, his eyes anxiously searching the shore for a sight of the golden cities of the Chinese. It was a tragic, unfulfilled voyage and the ships returned to England late in 1498. John Cabot died shortly afterward. He never knew that he had discovered North America for the English. The path of the Vikings led only to the New World.

The rest of the world quickly learned that all of the lands found by Colum-

bus, Cabot and Vespucci were not parts of Asia, but actually a new great land mass. When Balboa, in 1513, stood on a mountain top in Panama and saw the Pacific Ocean stretching to the horizon, it became a fact. The Spanish, for a while, were content to exploit their findings and build an empire, but other countries regarded the American continents as a nuisance, a blockade cutting across the sea lanes to Asia.

Many navigators felt that the way past

Were other routes to Asia explored?

the Americas lay to the north. There the continent is broken into large island masses with deep bays cutting into the mainland. Many plans were made for finding

The English navigator-explorer Henry Hudson sailed into New York harbor.

an open water passage and many expeditions set forth in search of one. John Cabot's son, Sebastian Cabot, made one such attempt. Two Portuguese expeditions led by the brothers Gaspar and Miguel Cortereal searched vainly among the bays and inlets of the northernmost reaches of the continent for what soon became known as the Northwest Passage.

Early in the seventeenth century the

What did Henry Hudson explore?

English navigator, Henry Hudson, made three determined efforts to find a way past North America. On his first voyage in 1607 he sailed up the east coast of Greenland past Spitsbergen until the polar ice stopped him. In 1609, this time sponsored by the Dutch East India Company, Hudson sailed his *Half Moon* into New York harbor and up the Hudson River all the way to the site of Albany before deciding he was on a river and not a passageway to China. Not at all discouraged by his previous failures, Hudson tried again in 1610. He was sailing for the English once more, in a ship proudly named *Discovery*. He passed through Davis Strait and entered Hudson Bay. This large body of water looked like the fabled Northwest Passage, but it only proved to be landlocked.

The search for a passage to Asia was one of the reasons for the exploration of North America. No one knew how broad the continent really was, and expeditions followed rivers and valleys in the hopes that they might reach the Pacific after a short journey, and perhaps even see Asia across a short strip of water! So strong was the dream of the fabled golden cities of the Khans that both explorers and kings refused to see the possibilities of the New World. It was only when the struggling colonies of the English and the Dutch began to show progress, and the riches of the Spanish empire shone in the capitals of Europe, that the Americas came to be regarded as more than just steppingstones to Asia.

Magellan and Cook Explore a New Ocean

The project was the same. The motive had not changed. Somehow a route to Asia had to be found by sailing westward. If the two newly discovered American continents had no natural passage to the Pacific Ocean, then a way must be found to sail around them. This project became the career of Ferdinand Magellan. It also brought about his death.

Magellan wanted to be able to reach the Spice Islands, or the Moluccas as we call them today, by sailing west. He

What was Ferdinand Magellan's plan?

Above is a portrait of the navigator Ferdinand Magellan, who led an expedition which succeeded in circumnavigating the world. The famous voyage of this Portuguese-born seaman gave proof that the earth is round. Unfortunately, Magellan was killed before the expedition was completed. The solid line on the map shows the course of his fleet while Magellan was still alive. The dashes show the continuation of the course after the explorer's early death in the Philippine Islands.

supposed it would be an easier trip than rounding Africa, passing India and making the passage through the Malay Straits. Like many navigators of his time, he thought the world to be much smaller than it is, with only a short journey to be made across the Pacific Ocean. He presented this scheme to the Portuguese court and was immediately refused. Magellan soon fell out of favor in his country and became a Spanish citizen shortly after. In Spain, he brought his plan to King Charles V.

In 1494, the rights to all of the non-Christian world had been awarded to Spain and Portugal by Pope Alexander VI in an effort to keep the two empire-building countries at peace with each other. This was accomplished by drawing an arbitrary line across a world map from north to south just east of North

Only the seaworthy ship *Victoria* returned to Spain.

America. Portugal was to own all the lands to the east of the line, and Spain all lands to the west. Fortunately for Portugal, the line crossed South America, leaving Brazil to the east. Magellan, who was using a globe as a map, drew the line all the way around the earth. Since no one was sure of the longitude

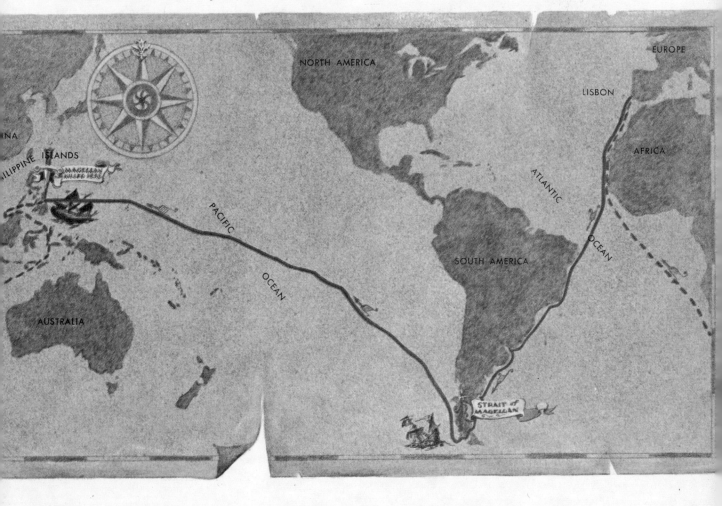

On April 27, 1521, Magellan landed with sixty men on Mactan, an island in the Philippines. An attack by natives on the outnumbered party ended Magellan's life.

of the Spice Islands, Magellan told the Spanish king that he would sail to the Spice Islands to determine if they fell within the Spanish zone. In addition, he proposed returning to Spain by continuing to sail west. This would prove once and for all that the earth was round.

King Charles accepted the plan and decided to pay the expenses for the expedition. From the very beginning the undertaking was a tragic venture. Five small ships were assigned to the navigator, the *Trinidad, San Antonio, Concepcion, Victoria* and *Santiago*. All were old and leaky. The crews were a rebellious lot and the Spanish captains commanding them resented taking orders from a Portuguese.

Was Magellan successful?

The course of Magellan's voyage and its highlights can be followed on the map (pages 40-41). He had to fight not only the elements, but his men as well. He succeeded in crushing a mutiny, though the *Santiago* was eventually lost, the *San Antonio* had deserted and Ma-

gellan himself was finally killed in a battle with natives in the Philippines. But he completed at least part of his task — the world had been circumnavigated by a man.

After Magellan's death, the rest of the fleet continued the trip and reached the Spice Islands — which did lie within the Spanish half of the world — where they loaded their holds with rich goods. But only the *Victoria* proved seaworthy at this point and, under the command of Sebastian del Cano, it set sail across the Indian Ocean, past the Cape of Good Hope and home to Spain. It arrived on September 8, 1522, the first vessel in history to sail around the world. Of the 230 men, only 18 returned in the *Victoria*, but the daring navigator, Ferdinand Magellan, lay in an unmarked grave in the Philippines.

Magellan's voyage proved three things.

What did Magellan's epic voyage prove?

First, that the world was round. This was known in theory at the time, but the circumnavigation made the theory a fact. Second, that there was a passage past the Americas that led to Asia. Third, and perhaps the most ironic, Magellan proved that the greatest of all navigational geniuses, Prince Henry of Portugal, was right when he pointed out over a century earlier that it would be much easier to reach Asia by sailing around Africa. In addition, Magellan's feat opened the Pacific to further exploration.

More than two hundred years later, in 1768, Captain James Cook led an expedition into the Pacific. Perhaps for the first time in all recorded history, there was a new motive for exploration. Cook's expedition was for science, to increase human knowledge, and since that time, explorers have been closely linked with scientists instead of,

What was the importance of Captain Cook's expeditions?

as in the old days, economic conquest and empire-building.

Cook went to Tahiti with a group of scientists to observe the transit of the planet Venus across the sun. His other mission was geographical. He was to attempt to locate and map as many of the Pacific islands as possible, as an aid to future navigation. Cook's ship, the *Endeavour,* sailed over great stretches of the South Pacific during this voyage. New Zealand was visited and the long coastline of Australia was accurately mapped.

A second voyage took place in 1772. Cook commanded two ships, the *Discoverer* and the *Adventure.* His mission this time was to search for a great new continent south of Australia. He crossed the Antarctic Circle several times without once sighting Antarctica, but the voyage was not a total loss. Cook discovered many new island groups and he returned with maps and

Captain James Cook (1728-1779), the English navigator and explorer, is famous for three celebrated expeditions.

The map shows the routes of Cook's voyages. His first expedition (solid line) occurred in 1768-69; the second voyage (dashes), in 1772-74; third voyage (dots and dashes), in 1776. The trips were mainly scientific in aim.

RESOLUTION

Tahiti was one stop in Cook's South Pacific ventures.

tables of distance that were more accurate than ever before.

Cook's last voyage began in June, 1776.

What was the reason for Captain Cook's last voyage?

This mission was historic—to find the fabled Northwest Passage. The search for this mythical waterway had long since been abandoned, but the British government was curious to see if there really was such a passage. Cook elected to try from the west and he piloted the *Discoverer* and *Resolution* around the Cape of Good Hope, through the Indian Ocean and out into the Pacific. There he turned north, revisiting many of the islands he had discovered earlier and rediscovering the Sandwich or Hawaiian Islands. He sailed up to the tip of Alaska and passed through the Bering Straits into the Arctic Ocean, convinced that this, at last, was the elusive channel. Actually it was and still is, but the grinding floes of ever-frozen ice that grip the Arctic Ocean present a barrier that cannot be sailed through.

Cook returned to the Hawaiian Islands where, like Magellan, he lost his life in battle. He was the first of the modern scientist-explorers, an astronomer, a physician, a geographer — a man who sailed for knowledge.

To the Ends of the Earth — and Beyond

By the dawn of the nineteenth century, all but one of the major land masses on the earth had been discovered and fairly well mapped. Explorers were venturing into the interior areas of the huge continents, following rivers to their sources, discovering mountain ranges, finding strange tribal cultures. The two major areas left for the questing explorers were the polar regions. It was suspected that a huge continent existed around the South Pole and the same conjectures applied to the North Pole. But there was another objective. Science had a great deal to gain from technical research done at the poles and, in the spirit of Captain James Cook, the explorers went forth to the ends of the earth. There was yet a third reason for the intense drive to the poles. It was pride. Every man who ventured into the icy seas wanted to be the first to stand at the apex of the earth, the most remote part of the planet.

Robert E. Peary made the first successful attempt to reach the North Pole. But this should not be regarded as a lone effort. All polar expeditions had to rely on the information gathered by earlier

Who was the first man to reach the North Pole — and when?

groups and the discovery of the pole came as a result of the accumulation of knowledge. Peary had made several treks across the polar ice in the latter half of the nineteenth century. Disasters were frequent and he escaped with his life from many dangerous situations. However, like all true explorers, he was always willing to place his life in jeopardy to discover the unknown. His final attempt was made in 1908. The ship *Roosevelt* was sailed to Cape Sheridan and then Peary led his party on foot. Nineteen sleds and 133 dogs brought the supplies across the ice floes and by April 6, 1909, Peary, his aide Henson and four Eskimos stood on top of the world. Soundings proved that no land existed there. The Arctic Ocean, cov-

The nuclear-powered sub *Skate* reached the North Pole from the east, July 30, 1958.

Robert Falcon Scott's ill-fated party reached the South Pole on January 18, 1912. But this heroic group perished returning to their base.

ered by its eternal ice, was the site of the North Pole. After planting the American flag, Peary led his small party back along the many dangerous miles to his ship. One of the most remote parts of the world had been touched by man.

One of the greatest polar achievements came in the year 1958. The age-old dream of finding a Northwest Passage was finally realized! On August 3, 1958, the United States atomic submarine *Nautilus* reached the pole by water. True, it was several hundred feet below the pole, submerged deep in the Arctic Ocean, but it crossed the pole from the west and continued toward the east, emerging in the Greenland Sea. This was a true passage — the first made by ship — and in the future, cargo submarines may use this route as a standard connecting link between the Atlantic and Pacific oceans. Just several days after the trip of the *Nautilus,* the atomic submarine *Skate* approached the pole from the east and actually managed to surface there at the top of the world.

In what way was the Northwest Passage found?

Throughout the same long period that saw the gradual conquest of the North Pole, the southern polar region was also a subject of intense interest. Captain Cook's reports of the existence of huge herds of seals and whales in the southern seas attracted fishermen from many countries. This abundance of attention naturally led to exploration. The first man to see the Antarctic continent itself was William Smith, a member of the crew of the British ship *Williams,* in February, 1819. In 1820, Edward Bransfield became the first to actually chart a section of the mainland.

Why were several nations interested in the Antarctic?

Then the expeditions followed thick and fast. The Russians and Scandinavians, as well as the British, made determined efforts at exploration, but many other countries joined the search also. Men like Weddell, d'Urville, Wilkes and Ross were responsible for the early charting of the seas and coastlines of Antarctica. Then came the push to the South Pole. It is a heartbreaking history, for many expeditions disappeared

in the grim whiteness and never returned.

The most dramatic story is that of Captain Robert Falcon Scott of the British Navy. After some preliminary explorations, he sailed for Antarctica in 1910 with full intentions of pushing on to the South Pole. His party reached the pole on January 18, 1912. Then came the great disappointment.

Who discovered the South Pole?

At the pole they found the markers of the first discoverer. It was the Norwegian explorer Roald Amundsen who had been there on October 20, 1911. With heavy hearts and bleak discouragement, Scott and his four companions, Wilson, Bowers, Oates and Evans, started the long, lonely trek back to their base. The weather was completely against them. Icy cold had descended on the whole continent and Evans quietly died on the Beardmore glacier. Oates showed the world the utmost of human nobility by walking out into a blizzard when he realized that there was not enough food left for all of them.

Rescue parties found Scott, Wilson and Bowers frozen to death in their tiny tent. Scott's beautifully written diary told the whole tragic story.

Of what interest is the South Pole in our own time?

Admiral Byrd flew over the pole in 1929 and then established a series of bases for scientific observation. These bases were maintained for many years and expanded recently as part of the International Geophysical Year. Scientists from all over the world are now discovering many of the secrets of nature formerly locked in the eternal ice.

The most recent exploit to take place on the Antarctic continent happened in 1958. A party commanded by Sir Vivian Fuchs and Sir Edmund Hillary, the conqueror of Mount Everest, crossed the continent in a trek that lasted from November 27, 1957 to March 2, 1958. The twelve-man expedition, driving specially built vehicles, toiled across the mountains, glaciers and plateaus. They passed the South Pole on their way, but the main purpose was to map the area and take geologic soundings.

No one knows what more may be discovered in Antarctica. This land mass, probably rich in minerals, may well remain locked in ice until man learns to control the weather.

What are the new frontiers in exploration and discovery?

There are now two directions left for explorers — down into the depths of the sea, and up into the infinite regions of space. An important event in deep-sea exploration oc-

A futuristic view: lunar base with rocket launchers.

curred on January 23, 1960 when two men descended in the bathyscaphe *Trieste* to the ocean floor itself. Their vehicle, a sort of underwater dirigible, sank into the Mariana Trench in the Pacific Ocean and reached a depth of almost seven miles. It was an international expedition. The bathyscaphe was designed by a Frenchman, August Piccard, and manned by his son Jacques and Lieutenant Don Walsh of the United States Navy. This was the deepest dive ever recorded, but it will be followed by others.

Both the United States and the Soviet Union have begun to explore space, the most exciting frontier ever to face man. Already many satellites circle the earth. Satellites are in a sun orbit and a rocket has hit the moon.

On April 12, 1961, Major Yuri Gagarin, a Russian pilot, was launched from the Soviet Union in a five-ton space vehicle. He was the first man to orbit the earth. His craft, controlled from the ground, circled the earth in 89.1 minutes.

On May 5, 1961, Navy Commander Alan B. Shepard Jr. of the United States was launched from Cape Canaveral, Florida in a 2,000-pound Mercury capsule. The craft reached a 115-mile height, and was man's first pilot-controlled flight in outer space.

But man, after looking back at his whirling home, with its blue seas and green hills, will turn his face outward to the other planets. These are new lands to explore and beyond them, at distances so immense that the imagination is staggered by the very numbers, are the stars.

Some day, far in the future, counterparts of the great earlier explorers will set forth on the limitless sea of space. It is possible that circling the remote stars are planets containing other intelligent beings. They may even join our questing humans in the never-ending search for the unknown.

48

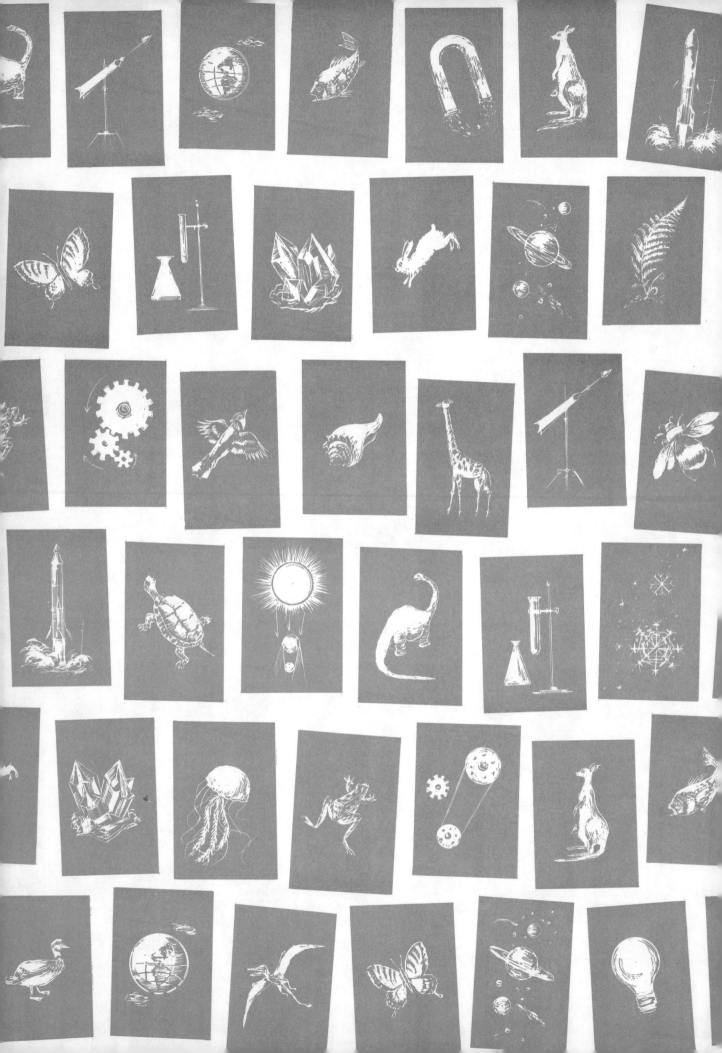